THE

Old Photographs

SERIES

LANCASTER AND THE LUNE VALLEY

A studio portrait c. 1896 by Platt Brothers of 7, Common Garden Street, Lancaster. The photograph is of Mrs Henrietta Dowthwaite (née Simpson), the author's grandmother.

THE

Old Photographs

SERIES

LANCASTER AND THE LUNE VALLEY

Compiled by

Robert Alston

CHALFORD

BATH • AUGUSTA • RENNES

First published 1994

The Chalford Publishing Company Limited
St Mary's Mill, Chalford, Stroud
Gloucestershire GL6 8NX

ISBN 07524 0015 0

Typesetting and origination by
Alan Sutton Limited
Printed in Great Britain by
Redwood Books, Trowbridge

Proclaiming the Fair, Lancaster.

Contents

The family of Richard and Mary Ann Alston, photographed by Alfred Millington of Halton, at their home at 2, New Street, Halton in 1904. Standing, left to right: Richard, John William, Alice Maud and Washington. Seated: Elsie, Mary Ann, Margaret Eleanor, Isabella Jane, and Norval Henry.

Carte de Visite photographed by J.N. Stockdale of 45 North Road, Lancaster, c. 1894.

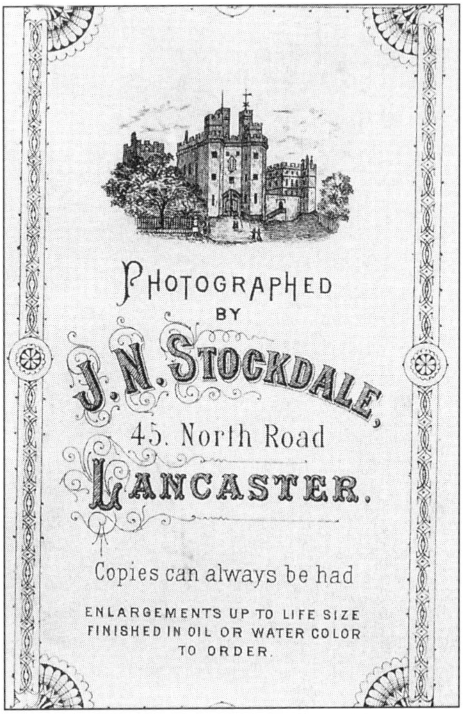

The reverse side shows a view of Lancaster Castle. Offers of enlargements to life size were commonplace and the work of artists emulated, with finishes in oil or watercolour.

Introduction

The photographs included in this book depict life principally in the first quarter of the twentieth century. They are a testimonial to those photographers who recorded the events of their time – street scenes, pageantry, disasters, and many other subjects that were captured for posterity.

The state entry into Lancaster of the High Sheriff, Mr Herbert Storey, in July 1904, the visit of Field Marshall Earl Roberts V.C. to dedicate the King's Own Royal Lancaster Regiment Memorial Chapel in the same month, the disastrous flooding of Lancaster and Morecambe in March 1907, the fire which destroyed the Athenaeum Theatre (built in 1781) in February 1908, H.M. King George V's visit to Lancaster in August 1912, and the Lancaster Pageant of August 1913, which captured the imagination of the entire area, were subjects faithfully recorded by local photographers.

The professional photographers in Lancaster are first recorded in the 1850s. They set up studios, partly because their equipment was both heavy and cumbersome. A typical advertisement of the time, appearing in the *Lancaster Gazette*, dated 21 April 1855, and placed by Mr R. Pateson, states:

"Portraits to life taken by the Daguerreotype, Calo-type, and Photographic Processes. Mr R. Pateson respectfully solicits parties requiring the likenesses of themselves or friends taken by the above processes, to apply at his apartment at Mrs Cass's, 87 Market Street, Lancaster, two doors above the King's Arms, where he flatters himself he will be enabled to give every satisfaction."

As the nineteenth century drew to a close, the number of photographic studios increased. Advertising for custom became commonplace and in 1896, for example, Robert Davis of 46 Church Street, Lancaster, guaranteed perfect satisfaction with Cartes de Visite costing from five shillings (twenty five present day pence) per dozen, and Cabinets from ten shillings per dozen.

An early pioneer of photography in Lancaster was Mr John Davis, who had premises initially in Alfred Street, and later in Market Street. The use of "wet plates" was superseded by the carbon process, which he introduced into Lancaster in 1874. In 1894 he was elected a Fellow of the Royal Photographic Society and was privileged to take photographs of local views which were presented in an album to the King and Queen when they visited Lancaster to open the Royal Infirmary in 1896.

The official approval of the picture postcard in September 1894 was to have a dramatic bearing on the industry, and although many of the early cards were designed and printed in Germany photographers were soon to appreciate the opportunities resulting from an increased demand for postcards at the turn of the century. Lancaster photographers prominent in the field at the time were George Howarth, Davis and Sons, and W. Johnston. Their work is well represented in this book, as is that of other unidentified photographers. Howarth, in particular, recognised the added interest in including people in his photographs, and he leaves a marvellous legacy for social historians.

Competition from photographers-publishers covering a wider area meant that there could be no relaxation by local photographers. Quality postcards of the North of England were produced by Matthews of Bradford, Turner of Skipton, A.E. Shaw of Blackburn, A.J. Evans of Preston, and many others. Major publishers produced postcards covering the entire country.

The reliability of the postal service was such that the postcard served the purpose of the telephone in today's environment. Postcards to trades people, written and posted in the morning, produced delivery of goods in the afternoon. Postcards written and posted mid-afternoon confirmed social and other arrangements for the evening of the same day – the postcard was indispensable.

The hobby of collecting postcards gained popularity, and photographers and publishers vied with each other, seeking to produce the most attractive cards. The vast quantity of early postcards which remain in existence owes much to this hobby, which remained popular up to the outbreak of the First World War. A significant revival of the hobby has taken place in the last few years.

The reader is invited to make the journey which represents my earliest recollection in the 1930s of visiting the area, although it is no longer possible to view the magnificent scenery from the comfort of a railway coach travelling on the Hellifield to Lancaster line of the Midland Railway. Parental confirmation that we are now in Lancashire greeted our arrival at Wennington Station. The station was a hive of feverish activity – railway staff inviting passengers to change for Carnforth, and porters on hand to assist with their luggage. Onward to Hornby, with views of the Rivers Wenning and Hindburn, and into the Lune Valley, eventually arriving at Caton.

The River Lune dominates the remainder of the journey through Halton to Lancaster Green Ayre Station, where sadly no trace of the railway can now be seen. Two restless boys alight, having spent the journey in competition instigated by their mother to be the first to spot one of Uncle Arthur Dowthwaite's coal wagons en route for, or returning from, the Yorkshire coalfield, carrying best Silkstone Nuts.

Released by our parents in Stonewell, we raced up Moor Lane, pausing breathless at the canal, and turned to appreciate the magnificent view of Lancaster Castle from this supreme vantage point. All these scenes, and many more, are portrayed in this book. It is my wish that the contents will revive old memories for the more senior of our citizens, and provide a meaningful background for their children and grandchildren, who have listened patiently to accounts of earlier years.

One

The River Lune and its Tributaries Wennington to Lancaster

WENNINGTON STATION photographed by C. Bull of Wray. An important junction on the Lancaster branch of the Midland Railway, with a branch line to Carnforth. The official opening of the line from Lancaster Green Ayre to Wennington was on Wednesday 31 October 1849, when at 1.00pm the director and his friends made the journey in seven carriages drawn by two engines. The station was decorated with flags and crowded with spectators.

WENNINGTON POST OFFICE and Grocery Store of Mr A. Middleton, photographed c. 1912. The store was eventually to suffer the fate that befell many in rural communities – closure, requiring the villagers to travel either to Lancaster or Carnforth.

WENNINGTON. An unattended horse and trap patiently awaits its owner outside the Foster's Arms Hotel (see page 12). The stone steps, from which the Post Office and Grocery Store derives its name, can be clearly seen to the right of the store.

FOSTER'S ARMS HOTEL, WENNINGTON, now a private house, photographed by Davis and Son, Lancaster. The sender of the postcard, posted 29 June 1907, complains about the weather and hopes for two fine days to finish hay making. The hotel was part of the Hornby Castle Estate, which was sold by auction on 30 November and 1 December 1938. It was withdrawn at £1,900 and subsequently sold privately. For a short time it became a milk bar.

WENNINGTON VILLAGE. An idyllic scene, with agricultural implements framing the farmhouse built in 1684, and tastefully extended in 1910. An electricity sub-station, now built on this site, detracts from what remains an otherwise traditional rural background.

WENNINGTON HALL, photographed in about 1908, was rebuilt by Colonel W.A.F. Saunders, who was high sheriff in 1862. His wife, Dorothy Morley, was descendant of the former owners of Wennington in 1360. The hall passed to their son, Mr Charles Morley Saunders, on the death of his father in 1879. It is now a residential school for secondary boys. The old trees at Wennington Hall, shown below, are little changed some ninety years later.

MELLING STATION on the Midland Railway branch line from Wennington to Carnforth. The station closed even earlier than the run down of the railway system that saw the closure of the Wennington to Lancaster Green Ayre route.

MELLING VILLAGE in 1907, with the elevated position of St Wilfrid's Church dominating the photograph. The church stands on a plateau which is an ancient earthwork known as Castle Mount.

MELLING POST OFFICE. L. Gibson, the grocer and provision dealer, was licensed to sell tobacco and available to meet the requirements of the village community, a facility no longer available today.

TATHAM RECTORY stands close to the River Wenning, at the rear of Tatham Church. A quiet backwater, the rectory gardens are as immaculate today as they were in 1908 when photographed by C. Bull of Wray.

HINDBURN FORCE, WRAY. A series of small waterfalls on the River Hindburn present a most attractive picture on this postcard posted in 1907.

THE RIVER ROEBURN AND QUARRY BRIDGE, WRAY. The Backsbottom quarries were at one time renowned for the quality of their stone and flags. Much of the paving laid in Lancaster was of flags produced from these quarries. Mr Kayss transported the flags to Lancaster, using four horses and carts all year round.

WRAY MILL, standing on the north side of the River Roeburn, is set in most picturesque surroundings. Now a private residence, it has seen numerous changes during its life. The mill was used for carding wool for the hatters, when a thriving hat-making trade existed in Wray. It was later to become a cotton mill, giving employment to the women and girls of Wray, but, following the decline of the cotton trade, served at various times as a bobbin mill and a silk mill. The mill was a major employer for the people of Wray; its declining fortunes led many people to leave the village in the nineteenth century. It reopened in 1870, rented by Messrs Davis and Conder, and was used for dressing silk.

WRAY VILLAGE, photographed from "Back o' Beck" by George Howarth of Lancaster. The card was posted on 24 December 1907. The single storey building, to be seen in the foreground on the extreme right, was the shop of William Kenyon, the last nailmaker in Wray. There were, at one time, several nailmakers in Wray, each tradesman employing up to seven men.

WRAY FROM TENTER HILL, photographed by C. Bull, photographer of Wray. The hill takes its name from the frames located there, which were used for stretching cloth during its manufacture. The River Roeburn can be seen in the foreground.

MAIN STREET, WRAY, a typical photograph by George Howarth of Lancaster, taken c. 1906. Howarth was a firm believer in enlisting the general public to appear in his photographs. George Miller, clog maker and village postman, from 1906 to 1925, can be seen in the foreground.

MAIN STREET, WRAY, c. 1905. Main Street has seen few changes this century, but the cottage on the far left, which was the old post office and shop, was demolished in 1907. The postmaster for some forty years, up to 1904, was Mr William Clucas.

NEWTON'S STORES AND CAFE, WRAY, built in 1746 and photographed early this century, with its early bow window, is readily recognisable today as the village shop and post office.

WRAY SCHOOL, photographed by Howarth c. 1905, with George Miller, clogmaker and village postman in the foreground. The school was founded and endowed in 1684 by Captain Richard Pooley, a native of Wray, and rebuilt in 1885. Captain Pooley left a sum of £20 towards the building of the school. He also bequeathed £200 to be paid to his trustees to buy land, the yearly interest, rents, profits, etc., to be paid to the schoolmaster. Education was free to every child in Wray, Roeburndale and Botton.

WRAY VILLAGE AND RIVER ROEBURN, photographed from "Back o' Beck". It is difficult, from the above photograph, to imagine the devastation which was to follow the cloudburst occurring at 6.30pm on 8 August 1967. The River Roeburn rose to a height of twenty feet, and the cottages shown on the left hand side of the road (below) were swept away, leaving a pile of mud and stones in Main Street. A further seven cottages were damaged beyond repair.

WRAY BRIDGE AND THE RIVER ROEBURN. The Wray flood, on 8 August 1967, swept away the parapet of the bridge, and the barn on the banks of the river was broken almost in two. The flood rendered 37 people homeless and caused serious damage elsewhere in the village. The bridge over the River Hindburn, on the Wray to Wennington road, was swept away. Emergency services responded magnificently – The Lancashire Rivers Board diverted the course of the river away from backs of houses (see opposite page, top picture), and the County Council completed the erection of a Bailey bridge over the River Hindburn by 13 August, some few days after the storms.

PLEASE OBEY THE
HIGHWAY CODE AT
ALL TIMES

START 9-00 a.m.

SUNDAY, MAY 26th

WRAY VILLAGE

21 WRAY | WRAY 21

BENTHAM ROUND TABLE

SPONSORED WALK
in aid of the
Wray Disaster Fund.

Remember ! Show this card to your sponsor as proof of miles walked.

Nº 1328

WRAY SPONSORED WALK

ORGANISED BY BENTHAM ROUND TABLE No. 346

OFFICIAL CHECK-POINT AND ROUTE CARD

Group ....O. A. P.....

Walker's Name ....R. Alston....

Address ....35 Hall Drive....
....Caton....

IMPORTANT

YOU MUST CARRY THIS CARD WITH YOU DURING THE WALK AND GET IT STAMPED AT EACH CHECK POINT

WRAY FLOOD – A NATIONWIDE DISASTER APPEAL. A nationwide appeal was launched on television by the Rev. J.H. Burkinshaw, and in little over a week the fund had topped £8,000. Week after week donations were received from individuals, organisations and societies. On Sunday 26 May 1968 a sponsored walk, organised by Bentham Round Table, took place. The initial poor weather on the day is thought to have deterred a number of walkers but, in spite of the rain and the mist, some 936 walkers started the 21 mile trek. The village policeman, Gerry Forrest, was the first inhabitant of Wray to complete the course. The initial estimate was that the walkers raised £4,500, but it was thought that the fund total might reach £5,000.

MAIN STREET, WRAY. The seventeenth- and eighteenth-century cottages make a charming picture, each one with its own individual quality. For the discerning visitor with an interest in architecture, many a happy hour can be spent examining buildings on the street terminating at the George and Dragon Hotel, shown below.

BUTT YEATES, HORNBY, on a postcard posted in 1906. The narrow road to the right of the building, carrying traffic to Lancaster, is now widened, and the entrance no longer faces the road. The cross base, opposite Butt Yeates, is a reminder of an ancient road to Roeburndale and the high fells.

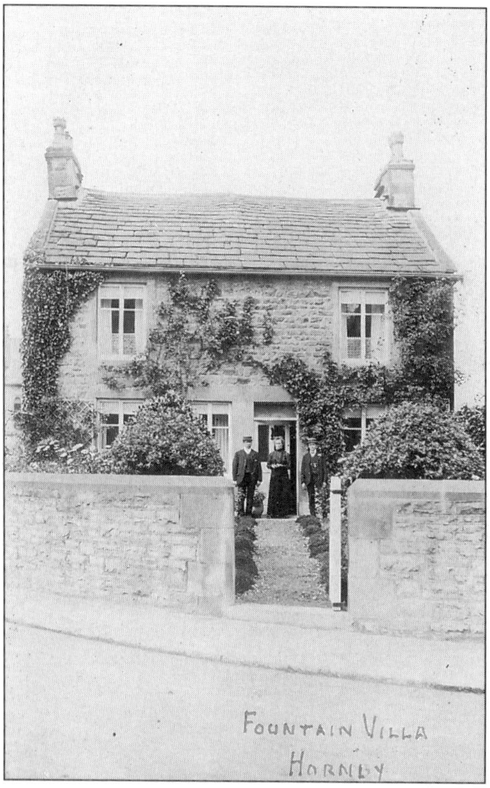

FOUNTAIN VILLA, HORNBY, the home of John Boardman, highway surveyor to the County Council for over thirty years.

A postcard of HORNBY INSTITUTE, postmarked 1915. The Institute was built in 1906 by Colonel William Henry Foster of Hornby Castle, and leased to the village trust.

HORNBY CASTLE, photographed by George Howarth of Lancaster c. 1904, standing high and overlooking the village, commands extensive views down the Lune Valley. Baines' *History of Lancashire* states that the site was occupied by the Romans. The Castle was purchased by John Foster Esq., a wealthy Bradford manufacturer, in 1861. He died in 1879 and was succeeded as Lord of the Manor by his son William, and subsequently by his grandson, Colonel William Henry Foster.

THE BRIDGE OVER THE RIVER WENNING, HORNBY. Schoolchildren were assembled on the bridge over the River Wenning to acknowledge the anniversary of the birth of Henry Cyril Warneford Foster, son of Colonel W.H. Foster. The event was recorded by a cannon salute – one shot for each year of the boy's age.

THE FOUNTAIN, HORNBY CASTLE, photographed in 1904 by Howarth of Lancaster, and a pictorial record of the children of Colonel and Mrs Foster. The daughters, Henrietta Marjory and Gladys Edith Foster, were keen horsewomen and were often to be seen riding through the village. Children attending Hornby School were taught at an early age the correct form of address whenever they rode by – the boys were to bow and the girls to curtsey.

THE FUNERAL OF COLONEL WILLIAM HENRY FOSTER OF HORNBY CASTLE. Colonel Foster died in 1908, at Algeciras in Spain, as a result of an attack of gout. Grandson of a wealthy industrialist employing 700 handloom weavers in Bradford, Colonel Foster maintained his interests in Yorkshire, in addition to those he undertook in Lancashire. He was Lord of the Honour and Manor of Hornby and the Manor of Tatham, Patron of the Livings of Hornby and Tatham, Trustee of the Living of Wray, and Member of Parliament for Lancaster Division, 1895-1900. He was a member of the 2nd West Yorkshire (Prince of Wales's Own) Yeomanry Cavalry for twenty-one years, which he commanded in 1891-92. A keen follower of the hunt, he was appointed Master of the Vale of Lune Harriers in 1890.

LOYAL NORTH LANCS AT HORNBY, 1910. During the uneasy peace prior to the First World War, the Lune Valley was much used by the army for training manoeuvres. The photograph shows the troops marching in the direction of Hornby.

CHURCH PARADE, 7 AUGUST 1910, HORNBY CAMP. Church parades were a feature of the summer training. The out barn to Lawnds Farm (now Holme Head Farm) can be seen in the background.

LANCE CORPORAL W.A. WILLIAMS at Hornby Camp in August, 1910. Horses played a significant role in manoeuvres, particularly in the transport of equipment (see below) to serve close on 6,000 men based at Hornby.

THE 4TH LOYAL NORTH LANCASHIRES are joined by the village people at Hornby for the church parade on 7 August 1910. The chaplain, Reverend L.D.W. Spencer M.A., can be seen in the centre of the group, and Lawnds House is in the background.

HORNBY CAMP, 1910. The 4th Loyal North Lancashires camp was located close to Lawnds Farm. The village of Gressingham can be seen in the background.

Hornby continued to be used by the army as a training ground after the First World War. The photograph is of a Field Ambulance Unit of the Royal Army Medical Corps, taken in 1923.

THE CASTLE INN, HORNBY, on a postcard postmarked 1905. A coaching inn, the Castle Hotel is on the Lancaster to Richmond turnpike road, which was authorised by statute in 1750. There is still much evidence of the turnpike along the Lune Valley, by way of coaching inns, toll houses and old milestones.

THE VILLAGE, HORNBY. A fine example of a milestone is to be seen on the right hand side of the road. St Margaret's Church, with its fine octagonal tower, is in the centre of the photograph. The tower was built in 1514 by Edward Stanley, Sheriff of Lancashire and created Lord Mounteagle by Henry VIII, for his part in the battle at Flodden Field in 1513. The remainder of the church is more modern, with rebuilding carried out in 1817 and 1889.

A bird's eye view of Hornby, taken from the tower of St Margaret's Church, with the Castle Hotel in the foreground and the River Wenning flowing to meet the Lune.

A postcard of THE CASTLE HOTEL, HORNBY and the bridge over the River Wenning, postmarked 1915. The bridge was later to be strengthened and widened to meet the increasing demands of road users.

VALE OF LUNE HARRIERS. The Vale of Lune Harriers were a familiar sight during the hunting season, which commences the first Saturday in October and runs through to the end of February in the following year. Founded in 1866, the Harriers were to be seen in an area including North Lancashire and the County of Westmorland, now part of Cumbria. The kennels were originally at Bentham but moved first to Melling and then to Hornby. The photograph above is dated 1906, when Colonel William Henry Foster of Hornby Castle was the Master of the Harriers. He was succeeded by his daughter, Miss Henrietta Marjory Foster. The hunt had many supporters in the area and the puppies were farmed out to farmers and followers, who cared for them and exercised them until they reached an age when they were ready for the kennels.

VALE OF LUNE HARRIERS MEET AT HORNBY.

A postcard of Hornby, taken from Wenning Bridge and postmarked 1906, with the once familiar scene of sheep being driven along the road. The photograph was taken c. 1904, prior to the building of Horby Institute.

THE VICARAGE, HORNBY, c. 1904, built in an age when size and heating costs were not a consideration. Not surprisingly, in view of the trend in the last decade, it is now a retirement home.

A postcard by Matthews of Bradford, featuring Holly House, the residence of the manager of Hornby Estate.

GRESSINGHAM, a charming unspoilt village. There now remains no evidence of Rose Cottage, which can be seen on the right of the photograph.

HORNBY STATION, on the Midland Railway line from Hellifield to Lancaster Green Ayre, opened in 1849. Following closure of the line, the track was removed in 1968. The station was located on the Farleton border.

THE TOLL HOUSE FILLING STATION, HORNBY, is to be found at Farleton, approximately half a mile from Hornby village. The house already standing on this site was ideally situated to become a toll house when the Lancaster to Richmond turnpike was authorised in 1750. In November 1816, James Swindlehurst, aged 70, keeper of the turnpike gate, was found drowned in the River Wenning.

CLAUGHTON OLD HALL. Visitors to this location today will be somewhat bemused to find only one wing of this fine building in situ. This wing is Claughton Hall Farm, and the remainder of the Hall is to be found high on the moor, where it was rebuilt in 1932-35 following dismantlement stone by stone. Some changes to the original were effected in the rebuilding, and a new upper Great Hall was formed.

CLAUGHTON OLD HALL. The church of St Chad can be seen to the left of the wall standing below the Hall. The church has a bell dated 1296 – the oldest dated bell in England.

BROOKHOUSE CHURCH, CATON, photographed c. 1908. Standing at the eastern end of the parish is St Paul's Church, occupying an elevated position. The tower is ancient but the remainder of the church was rebuilt in 1865-67. A twelfth-century doorway, the old church porch door, was incorporated in the building.

BROOKHOUSE, CATON, c. 1910, photographed by an unidentified photographer who was to faithfully record almost every part of the village. The bridge over Bull Beck can be seen in the foreground. Brookhouse is the second largest of the four centres of population comprising Caton, and until industrialisation was the focal point of village life.

BOLTON'S ROW, BROOKHOUSE, c. 1908. The Black Bull Inn on the right of the photograph, which was originally a farmhouse, is a sixteenth-century building. The bridge over Bull Beck is in the foreground, and a plague stone is built into the right hand parapet of the bridge.

OLD QUARRY, MOORSIDE, CATON, with the road leading to Littledale, the most sparsely populated part of Caton. Artle Beck, flowing through Littledale, provided the water power for the mills located at Town End. Coal and flint were worked in Littledale in the nineteenth century, and a disused brick works can still be seen on the road to Roeburndale.

MOORGARTH, CATON, is located at Moorside, Caton, and was originally the workhouse for the poor of Bolton-le-Sands, Borwick, Caton, Claughton, Farleton, Gressingham, Halton, Heysham, Hornby, Nether Kellett, Over Kellett, Poulton, Bare, Torrisholme, Quernmore, Roeburndale, Slyne with Hest, Tatham, Wennington, and Wray with Botton. It was considered capable of holding 150 paupers and was under the jurisdiction of a board of guardians who met monthly at the workhouse.

LITTLEDALE HALL, CATON, at the source of Artle Beck, occupies the most remote part of Caton. Formerly known as Tonguemore and standing in some 300 acres of ground, it was the home of the Dodson family. The Reverend John Dodson, who until 1849 was vicar of Cockerham, left the church and established a "free" church at Littledale from 1848 to 1908.

LITTLEDALE HALL.

HORNBY ROAD, CATON. Population growth in Caton reached a peak in the middle of the nineteenth century, and housing for mill workers was concentrated at Town End, close to the mill race flowing from Artle Beck. Further building along Hornby Road and Brookhouse Road (see below) was undertaken at the end of the nineteenth century. Houses built between 1950 and 1960 have now effectively linked the communities of Town End and Brookhouse, which were quite separate in 1912 when these photographs were taken.

BROOKHOUSE ROAD, CATON.

THE STAGE COACH AT CATON, c. 1905.

THIRLMERE BRIDGE, CATON. The bridge carrying the two pipelines supplying water from Thirlmere to Manchester is one of thirty three along the pipelines' entire length. The scheme involved raising the level of Thirlmere to provide 50 million gallons of water per day, for 160 days. The scheme was such that even if no rain fell during that period the water of the lake would not fall below its original level. Water was first supplied to the city on 12 October 1894.

THE VIADUCT OVER THE RIVER LUNE, CATON, carrying the Midland Railway line from Hellifield to Lancaster. Following the closure of the line, the track was uplifted in 1968. Walkers can now enjoy a pleasant stroll along the old line. The publisher of the postcard, which was posted in 1915, erroneously entitles it "Waterworks Bridge", as is shown in the photograph above.

STAGING POINT, STATION HOTEL, CATON. Horse drawn coaches and passengers were a familiar sight at Caton when this photograph was taken in 1908. The Station Hotel was a halt along the very popular scenic route from Lancaster to Kirkby Lonsdale. The Station Hotel, earlier known as the New Inn, was licensed in 1830 and by 1899 was boasting a bowling green as well as providing stabling. The sign, suspended from the bracket mounted on the hotel, confirms that the National Telephone Company had installed a telephone for public use.

FORGE, CATON, shows the cottages erected for the workers at Forge Mill, which was built in 1752. It was one of five mills at Townend, Caton, and although initially a forge, it was to serve for the production of silk, cotton, flax and bobbins at various times in its history. The postcard is dated 1911, at which time the mill was producing bobbins. Following its closure in 1931, it stood empty until the 1970s, when it was converted to housing.

MOOR PLATT, CATON, originally the home of Thomas Davidson Smith, a member of the yeoman family recorded as living at Wray in 1633. It was the home of Colonel Hibbert in 1912 when this photograph was taken. It was bought by Mr Jowett of Bradford in 1930, and later purchased by Lancashire County Council as a home for the elderly.

FORGE BRIDGE, CATON. Another postcard produced by the unidentified Caton photographer, with Jack and Marion providing further interest beside the stream bed. Close by, Artle Beck was diverted into a dam to provide power for Forge Mill and Rumble Row Mill. The stream from the dam flows part of its length underground, reappearing at Broadacre and on to Willow Mill, then again near Town End Stores, and finally to Low Mill where it eventually reaches the River Lune.

ARTLE BECK BRIDGE, CATON. Artle Beck is recorded in history as the location where a six foot high Roman milestone was found. The milestone was removed to Caton Hall, the home of Mr B.P. Gregson, but subsequently transferred to Lancaster Museum.

BROADACRE COTTAGES, CATON were built by Albert Greg of Escowbeck on the lane leading to Rumble Row Mill. There is now no trace of the mill – Caton Primary School was built on the ground where the mill formerly stood.

ROCK M'JOCK COTTAGES, CATON, are close by Willow Mill. There is more than one story as to how they were given this name. The most popular story is the one relating to the repetitive noise from the machinery at Willow Mill, which seemed to say "Rock M'Jock" over and over again.

GRASSYARD WOODS, CATON, and the beck fed by Foxdale and Udale Becks rising high on Blanch Fell, later to merge with Artle Beck and provide the water supply so essential for the mills at Town End, Caton.

GRASSYARD HALL, CATON, alternatively known as Gresgarth Hall, the name favoured by Ordnance Survey, stands on the site of a much earlier building, alleged to have been built in the twelfth century. It has been rebuilt and added to at various times; the south-west wing was added in 1805. In 1802, a pit was sunk near the hall and, for a time, coal was extracted. The working was eventually abandoned, and attempts to identify coal deposits elsewhere in the area produced no success.

WESLEY ROW, CATON was built for mill workers, by the manager William Stubbs, in 1838. The Methodist Chapel is close by. The first house on the right was the first Co-operative store to open in Caton.

CYCLE PARADE, CATON GALA. The revival of Caton Gala in 1908 was to prove extremely popular with the village residents and drew support from the surrounding district. The fancy dress cycle parade was to be an annual feature of the gala. Other events included children's sports, sheep dog trials, wrestling, and an ambulance competition for a cup presented by Mrs Foster of Hornby Castle.

THE CYCLE PARADE AT CATON GALA IN JUNE 1909 attracted some 2,000 spectators. The ingenuity displayed by the female entrants to the parade provided an intriguing contest. Twenty contestants took part and, after great deliberation, the judges made the following awards: Ladies' First Prize to Miss May Cook, attired as an Egyptian; second prize to Miss Amy Fearing, who represented Lifebuoy Soap and had a lifebuoy slung round her shoulders; third prize to Miss May Muncaster, who, in a star spangled black costume, made a very artistic representation of "night". A special prize was awarded to Miss May Croft, who, as "Billiards up to date", carried a small but complete billiards outfit on her cycle. Two prizes were awarded to the gentlemen's section: first prize to J. Goodwin, "Red Indian"; second prize to J. Parker, "Monkey Brand Soap". The report of the gala includes details of the skipping rope competition, won by a girl of about 12 years. She accomplished the remarkable feat of skipping 1,460 times, and retired "as fresh as a daisy".

ESCOW COTTAGE LODGE, CATON, on a postcard dated August 1915, and (below) ESCOWBECK COTTAGE, the home of Albert Greg, cotton manufacturer, who died in 1910. The Greg family, already established as millers since 1784 at Quarry Bank Mill at Styal in Cheshire, purchased Low Mill at Caton in 1817. John Greg moved to Escowbeck Cottage in 1826. New Escowbeck was built in 1842, and landscaping to the grounds carried out, to eliminate the view of cottages at Town End. John Greg died in 1882, and the running of the mill passed to his son Francis, who died in 1901.

THE OLD OAK TREE, TOWN END, CATON.

Old Oak
Caton

THE POST OFFICE, CATON, and the lane to Caton Railway Station, once busy with passengers hurrying to catch the train to Lancaster Green Ayre, to their place of employment or to the shops. A special outing for the family would be to Morecambe for a day at the beach. Morecambe, on Saturday evenings, was also the destination for the young and unattached to enjoy the delights of the dance floor.

THE POST OFFICE, HORNBY ROAD, CATON, and a view of the home of the author's great grandmother, Mrs Amelia Purchase, prior to its incorporation in the shop in the centre of the photograph. The grocery store in the centre of the photograph also included a cafe, where refreshments could be obtained on the upstairs floor. The shop on the right, alongside which stands the horse drawn cart, was the store of Mr S. Proctor who, until 1904, had the grocery store at Town End, Caton.

THE HUNT MEETS AT THE STATION HOTEL, CATON. Hunting was a popular pursuit, and the Vale of Lune Hunt met regularly at the Station Hotel. The Hotel, licensed in 1830, went originally under the name "New Inn".

ARRIVAL OF THE 5TH LANCASHIRE REGIMENT AT CATON, 1910. The photograph shows the troops' arrival, and marching from Caton Railway Station. Two thousand, three hundred and forty one men were based in Caton for the annual camp in 1910. They were members of the 4th and 5th South Lancashire Regiments, together with the Liverpool Scottish Regiment, who made a fine sight in their kilts.

CATON CAMP and (below) CHURCH PARADE, CATON. The 5th South Lancashire Regiment, together with the 9th Liverpool Rifles, were based in fields near to Brookhouse. The 5th South Lancashires were under the command of Colonel R.W.H. Thomas. Their headquarters were at St Helens and included two companies: one from Prescot and one from Widnes. There was also a small detachment of men from Rainhill and Haydock.

GRASSYARD LODGE, CATON, provides us with another glimpse of Jack and Marion, who were frequently available to provide a little life for the photographer. Readers can place their own interpretation on the comment written by the sender, "Rather jolly up there in summer". The lodge gates were normally closed, and the lodgekeeper was always on hand to open the gates for horse drawn vehicles calling at the Hall.

THE OLD OAK TREE, CATON. A resident takes a rest on the stone steps where the monks laid out their Lune salmon for sale. The old oak tree, now but a shadow of its former self, today has the assistance of a support. The single storey building was once a smithy and the building to the right was occupied by one of a number of clogmakers at Town End. The last clogmaker to occupy the building was Joe Barton.

TOWN END, CATON, the most frequently photographed location in the village, with the old oak tree and grocer's shop occupied in succession by Samuel Bannister, Samuel Proctor and William Brodrick. The postcard is undated, but the grocer's name, S. Proctor, above the store, confirms the date of the photograph to be prior to 1904.

TOWN END, CATON, photographed in 1904. The new occupant of the grocery store, William Brodrick, appears at the doorway for inclusion in the photograph. There is no shortage of onlookers to make a balanced picture. The store was to remain in the hands of the family some sixty one years, Mrs Margaret Eva Parker succeeding her parents.

TOWN END, CATON, photographed c. 1910 (above) and in 1926 (below), showing little structural change in the buildings, and before any of the demolition which took place at a later date. The telegraph pole, in the foreground of the photograph below, heralds the advance of science. The grocer's shop has progressed to the point of newspaper boards providing the day's news as an incentive to encourage sales. The Ship Inn has passed from the hands of Charles Hodgson to the Lancaster Brewery of Yates and Jackson. Mine host at the Ship Inn, Mr Robert Sayce, stands at the edge of the road, passing the time of day with the stationary motorcyclist.

TOWN END, CATON, c. 1910, where many of the requirements of the mill workers were met. The grocery store of William Brodrick, providing provisions and teas for those travelling between Lancaster and Kirkby Lonsdale, was sadly demolished in January 1994, and is destined to become a parking area for the Ship Inn, the next building on the left. Charles Hodgson was mine host at the Ship Inn in the days of home brewed ales; the malt house, where brewing took place, is to the left of the inn. Next door is the clog maker, one of the three at Town End. A butcher's shop at the end of the row completes the picture.

THE OLD OAK TREE AND SILVER STREET, CATON, photographed in 1905 by George Howarth of Lancaster. Mrs Brodrick is standing in the doorway of the grocery store. The street lamp, fixed by bracket to the side of the store and installed by Mr Albert Greg of Escowbeck, was the first in Caton. The villagers celebrated by dancing beneath the light on the first day it was lit. Alice and Annie Gibson can be seen framed in the doorway of the cottage, partly screened by the old oak. Maggy Denny's house, in the background with the canopy above the door, was the first newspaper shop in Caton. Three small windows beneath the eaves of this house provided light for lacemaking.

MIDLAND RAILWAY STAFF AT CATON STATION, c. 1914.

LOW MILL, CATON, and the last opportunity to take a look at Jack and Marion – the latter almost buried beneath her large hat. The mill, built in 1784, differed from many of the mills in the area, which were required to change their products in the light of economic circumstances, by producing cotton throughout its working life. Much of the original mill was destroyed by fire in December 1837, and that shown in the photograph is the result of rebuilding in 1838. The mill was powered by water from the mill race running from Artlebeck into a large mill pond. The mill closed in 1970 and is now undergoing renovation into housing, the mill chimney having been dismantled.

BANK HOUSE, CATON, photographed in 1914, was the home of the manager of Low Mill. The house stands at the side of the mill pond, which was developed as a trout fishery after the mill closed. The building complex also included an apprentice house, built for the child labour which comprised much of the total labour force.

THE MIDLAND STATION, CATON. This postcard, published by A.J. Evans of Preston, is a good example of the fine quality of postcards published by this company. Although, at first glance, the scene appears deserted, two faces peer from the signal box looking in the direction of the photographer.

CATON VILLAGE. An early view of Town End, photographed by George Howarth of Lancaster, c. 1902. It is one of a number of his photographs of the village, and is entitled "Caton village, Lancaster No. 1".

PENNY BRIDGE, CATON. The earliest bridge over the River Lune, linking Caton and Halton, was built in 1806. This bridge collapsed, and was replaced by the Penny Toll Bridge, shown in the photograph, in 1883. Travellers continued to use the ford – the way prior to erection of the bridge – in order to avoid payment of the toll. Crossing the Lune by way of the ford was at times hazardous, and there are records of people drowning when attempting the crossing.

CROOK O' LUNE, CATON, with Penny Bridge and the railway viaduct in the background. Painted by Turner, and its beauty acknowledged by the poets Thomas Gray and William Wordsworth, its popularity with visitors has in no way diminished over the years.

BERRY COTTAGES, CATON, and Escow Beck, which forms the parish boundary, flowing to meet the Lune in the foreground. A row of beehives, once a familiar sight in rural communities, can be seen in the garden of one of the cottages.

BRITISH RAIL LIST OF TOLLS, HALTON. This photograph, taken in 1966, shows the toll levied for crossing Lune Bridge. The bridge, built by the Midland Railway, was taken over by British Rail on nationalisation of the railways.

LUNE BRIDGE AND WEIR, HALTON. The bridge, erected by the railway company, provided access from Halton village to the railway station. Tolls were levied and collected by railway personnel. In 1965, Lunesdale Rural District Council requested, without success, that the bridge be purchased by Lancashire County Council. The Rural District Council asked for this decision to be reviewed in July 1967 as there was a danger of vehicles exceeding four tons using the bridge when it was unmanned. Tolls were demanded only occasionally following the closure of the Lancaster–Wennington railway line.

THE TOLL BAR, BULK, photographed in 1966, the home of the author's great great grandfather in the 1870's. The traveller along the Lancaster to Richmond turnpike at that time would, in all probability, see men dressing stone for road repairs on land adjacent to the toll house. The triangular piece of ground on the opposite side of the lane was the garden for the toll house, and here soft fruit for sale in Lancaster market was grown.

HALTON. The photograph is taken from the platform of Halton Station, c. 1911. The Midland Railway board, listing the toll charges for Halton Bridge, can be seen in the foreground. The rear of the Greyhound Hotel on Low Road can be seen on the right of the photograph. The houses on Low Road, to the left of the hotel, are now demolished.

HALTON ROCKS, photographed by George Howarth.

S PHOTO G.H

CADETS' CAMP, HALTON, 1910. The 1st Liverpool Cadets, comprising eight officers, eighteen sergeants, and ninety-nine men, were based at Halton for their week's training in 1910. The Cadets, all gentlemen's sons, were required to pay their own expenses for the week. Their ages ranged from 12 to 17 years, and on reaching the latter age they entered various branches of the Territorial and Naval forces. During the week, they adopted the role of an enemy force for the Liverpool Brigade, taking up positions at Nether Kellett.

HALTON WATER on the River Lune, a popular boating rendezvous for the young and energetic. Halton Church tower can just be identified behind the trees on the bank of the river.

HALTON, photographed by Matthews of Bradford, the postcard posted in 1922. The toll bridge over the River Lune can be seen in the middle distance. The platform and buildings of Halton Railway Station, on the far bank of the river, merge with the hills in the background.

SMOLT MARKING, FORGE WEIR, HALTON, 1914. The photograph shows the Lune Board of Conservators involved in the marking of the young salmon. A paragraph in the *Lancaster Gazette* dated 16 September 1826 reports that upwards of 1,300lb weight of fine salmon were caught in the fishery of R.F. Bradshaw Esq. of Halton, in the first two days of that week.

THE BOAT HOUSE, HALTON, is situated on the banks of the River Lune at Halton Hall. To the left of the boat house is Tower House, built in the middle of the eighteenth century and part of the buildings belonging to Halton Hall. The boathouse was converted into a dwelling during the 1930s.

HALTON HALL, the home of Edmund Sharpe, Lord of the Manor of Halton. The hall has been the subject of much rebuilding during its life, and the building shown on the photograph would have borne little resemblance to the one occupied by Thomas Whitehead, the acting rector of Halton, during the seventeenth century. The hall is assured of its place in history as a result of occupation by successive generations of the Carus family, supporters of the Jacobite cause. When the Jacobite army reached Kirkby Lonsdale in 1715, Thomas and Christopher Carus, together with their father, all Papists, joined them to advise them that Lancaster was ill prepared to meet the advancing army.

ST WILFRID'S CHURCH, HALTON, the oldest part of which is the tower built in the sixteenth century. The remainder of the church was pulled down in 1792 and rebuilt. This part of the church was in its turn demolished and rebuilt in 1877. The photograph by George Howarth is dated c. 1904, prior to the erection of the lych gate in 1907. The houses on Church Street, on the left hand side of the photograph, are now demolished.

"THE RECTORY, HALTON" is the title given by George Howarth to this postcard, posted in 1907. Residents will recognise it as a photograph of the Manor House, but Howarth can be forgiven for his mistake, as it was at that time the home of John Harold Hastings, who was not only the Rector of Halton but also the Patron.

SKERTON PARK. James Williamson, the Liberal M.P. for Lancaster, was elevated to a peerage in 1895, selecting as his title Baron Ashton of Ashton. In addition to Williamson Park, which bears his name, he was also to provide funds for other ventures in Lancaster. These included the landscaping of the Lunesdale Gardens at Skerton, a popular riverside walk much appreciated by the residents. Lord Ashton was particularly generous to the residents of Skerton, distributing coal to the needy and also inviting them to a party held on his birthday.

AQUEDUCT BRIDGE OVER THE RIVER LUNE, LANCASTER. A favourite spot for boating activities is depicted on this postcard published by A.J. Evans of Preston. The bridge carries the canal, the Lancaster to Preston section of which was opened in 1792. Extensions northward were commenced under the direction of Mr William Cartwright, appointed resident engineer to the Lancaster Canal Company in 1794. He was the engineer in charge of the building of the Lune Aqueduct, which was opened in 1797.

THE LUNE, FROM SKERTON GARDENS, LANCASTER, with a view of the aqueduct bridge in the background.

LADIES' WALK, LANCASTER runs from the Lancaster side of Skerton Bridge – a popular walk alongside the River Lune and the northern section of the old mill race.

Two

Lancaster Bailrigg to Skerton Bridge

LANCASTER FROM THE SOUTH. Fine views of Lancaster can be obtained from many vantage points, and the two photographs on this page are probably the most popular, reflecting the commanding position of the Castle and the Parish Church. The views from the Parish Church are just as impressive, with Morecambe Bay and the Lune estuary in the foreground, and, in the distance, Cumbria and the magnificent mountains of the Lake District. The postcards are both published by A.J. Evans of Preston.

OLD BRIDGE AND VICAR'S FIELD, LANCASTER.

BAILRIGG, LANCASTER, photographed in 1912, the home of Sir Thomas Storey, who died in 1898, and, subsequently, his son, Herbert L. Storey (1853-1919). Storeys of Lancaster were founded in 1848, making table baize in a small workshop located on St George's Quay, Lancaster. A major employer in the town, they showed initiative in promoting new products to maintain the company's viability. They were in the foreground in the manufacture of plastic material from the early 1950s. In 1962 the Bailrigg estate was sold by the owners, Mr and Mrs Barton Townley, to provide the land on which Lancaster University was built.

THE HUNTING STABLES, BAILRIGG.

SCOTFORTH VILLAGE, and a view of the A6 looking south, on a postcard dated 1906. The post office, 92 Scotforth Road, still survives, as does the row of houses beyond (94-110 Scotforth Road). The houses beyond, at the extreme left of the photograph, have been demolished. A passing point for the trams can be seen in the foreground.

SCOTFORTH, and a view looking north towards Lancaster. The buildings on the left hand side of the road are recognisable as those in the photograph above. The building on the left has been demolished. A supermarket stands on the site of the buildings immediately behind the group of boys standing in the road. The driver of the tram takes advantage of the opportunity to appear in the photograph.

SCOTFORTH, photographed from Scotforth Square. The postcard above was posted in 1906, and the same scene, on the postcard below, posted in 1908. Scotforth, at that time, had not been entirely embraced by Lancaster, and there was open ground beyond St Paul's Church, Scotforth. The group above, intent on appearing in the photograph, are oblivious to the arrival of the tram at its Scotforth terminus. The tram service from Castle Station to Scotforth, run by Lancaster Corporation Tramways, opened in January 1903.

SCOTFORTH.

FLOWER STALL, SOUTH ROAD, LANCASTER.

THE
ROYAL LANCASTER INFIRMARY
FLOWER SATURDAY.
PLEASE PURCHASE
SCOTFORTH SCHOOL.
SOUTH ROAD.

LANCASTER CORPORATION TRAMWAYS CAR en route from Castle Station to Scotforth. The cars were built by the Lancaster Railway Carriage and Wagon Company Ltd. in 1902, and provided a fine spectacle in their chocolate and primrose colours.

BAY VIEW TERRACE, BOWERHAM, photographed by Robert Davis, the postcard bearing the date 1907. Street scenes were a common feature around this time, as photographers sought to increase their sales to the occupiers of the properties. This view is close by Davis's home at 45 Coulston Road.

Previous page: The photograph shows Scotforth School raising funds for the Royal Lancaster Infirmary on Flower Saturday.

SOUTH ROAD, LANCASTER, and a group of children gather outside the shop of N.R. Clifton, stationers and general dealers.

THE POINTER, LANCASTER, which marks the old boundary of the town, photographed by George Howarth of Lancaster, who has not missed the opportunity to include a group of children in the photograph. Centre piece is the lighting standard on which the signpost is mounted, showing the road to Wyresdale on the right. The road straight ahead is signposted to Kendal and Windermere.

LANCASTER BARRAGKS at Bowerham were erected in 1876-80, as headquarters of the 3rd (Reserve) Battalion of the King's Own Royal Lancaster Regiment. The Regiment was raised in 1680, under the title of the Second Tangier Regiment, and had various titles until 1715 when "The King's Own" was conferred upon it by King George I. The barracks were eventually to be taken over by St Martin's College. The postcard was posted in 1905.

LANCASTER BARRACKS – THE KEEP, which was eventually to be used as a library by St Martin's College.

NO. 4 REGIMENTAL DISTRICT STAFF, photographed in 1905 by W.G. Webber of Brock Street, Lancaster.

B BLOCK, BOWERHAM BARRACKS, LANCASTER.

PENNY STREET BRIDGE AND THE CANAL, LANCASTER. Whether by accident or design, two trams have been captured by the photographer as they cross the bridge. Bryant and May's matches, once a household name, are advertised on one of the trams. The hotels, White Cross Hotel and Corporation Hotel, will be unfamiliar to the majority of Lancastrians, as they have been renamed respectively Farmers'Arms and Alexandra Hotel. The two inns were originally owned by the Corporation.

A CARRIAGE OUTING FROM THE CORPORATION HOTEL, LANCASTER. The proprietor, William Dalzell Jackson, was not slow to recognise progress and, in addition to advertising Yates and Jackson's noted Lancaster ales and stout on his inn sign, offered accommodation for motorists and cyclists. The large yard and stabling for twenty eight horses was retained for the more conventional transport of the day.

THE ALEXANDRA HOTEL, LANCASTER in a more leisurely age, when travellers taking the A6 road north proceeded along Thurnham Street, rather than by way of King Street on the one way system which exists today.

KING STREET, LANCASTER, photographed in 1904, with Lancaster Corporation tram No. 2 just passing Corn Market Street, and about to turn into Common Garden Street. The shop of J. Wilson, grocer and provision dealer, is on the corner of King Street and Common Garden Street. On the left is the shop of Johnson and Sons, selling tapestries and wallpapers, and advertising the newest designs in draperies, blinds, curtains and coverings.

TOP OF MARKET STREET, LANCASTER, showing Scott's Temperance Hotel, now demolished. The Lancaster Temperance Society was formed in 1833, when alcoholism was of serious concern. The society drew popular support, despite opposition which sometimes resulted in violence. Several disturbances at temperance tea parties led to ten anti-teetotallers being brought before the magistrates in 1834, charged with creating a riot at a meeting held in a room in Mary Street. Eight of the defendants were found guilty and bound over to keep the peace and, also, to pay costs.

CHURCH STREET, LANCASTER, photographed with the *Guardian* newspaper offices on the far left, and the Nag's Head Hotel further down on the same side. The open air market, with its array of carts and produce, is traditionally held on Wednesdays and Saturdays.

PENNY STREET AND A LITTLE BIT OF OLD LANCASTER, photographed in 1905. The buildings shown on this photograph are now all demolished. The location is the junction of King Street and Penny Street, with the premises of H. Warbrick, painter and decorator, at 103 King Street on the extreme left. The clog maker's sign hangs outside James Cragg's shop on Penny Street. The hoarding advertises the entertainment alternatives: *The grip of the law*, by Fred Moule, and the L.D. Nicholls Company at the Athenaeum (The Grand Theatre, St Leonardgate), and the Lancaster Male Voice Choir's second annual concert at the Palatine Hall, to be held on Wednesday, 22 February, 1905. The Choir were supported by Miss Cassidy's string orchestra.

CHEAPSIDE, LANCASTER.

PENNY STREET, LANCASTER, with Boots the Chemist's shop entrance on the corner of Brock Street just identifiable on the right of the photograph. The studio of W.G. Webber, the Lancaster photographer at No. 1 Brock Street, was situated on the first floor, above the chemist's shop.

PENNY STREET, LANCASTER, with Whewell and Holmes, grocers, at 62-64 Penny Street and John Duxbury, picture framer and gilder, at 60 Penny Street.

PENNY STREET, LANCASTER, viewed from Horse Shoe Corner. The Queen's Hotel and the Bear and Staff Hotel are the two buildings immediately on the left. They were both coaching inns and the Bear and Staff had a life sized effigy of a bear and staff mounted over the doorway. "Next" now occupy the shop on Horse Shoe Corner.

MARKET STREET, LANCASTER, photographed by George Howarth of Lancaster. The postcard is dated 1905. In the right foreground is the ladies and gentlemen's hairdressers, Slater and Son – established for over sixty years and claiming to be specialists in artistic and ornamental hair-work. The horse drawn cart stands at the New Inn entrance. The old coaching inn dates back to 1767. It was bought by Mitchells, the Lancaster brewery company, in 1874, and their brewery was built between the New Inn and Church Street in 1880.

THE OLD TOWN HALL, MARKET STREET, LANCASTER.

MARKET STREET, LANCASTER.

PRATTS
SPIRIT
OILS

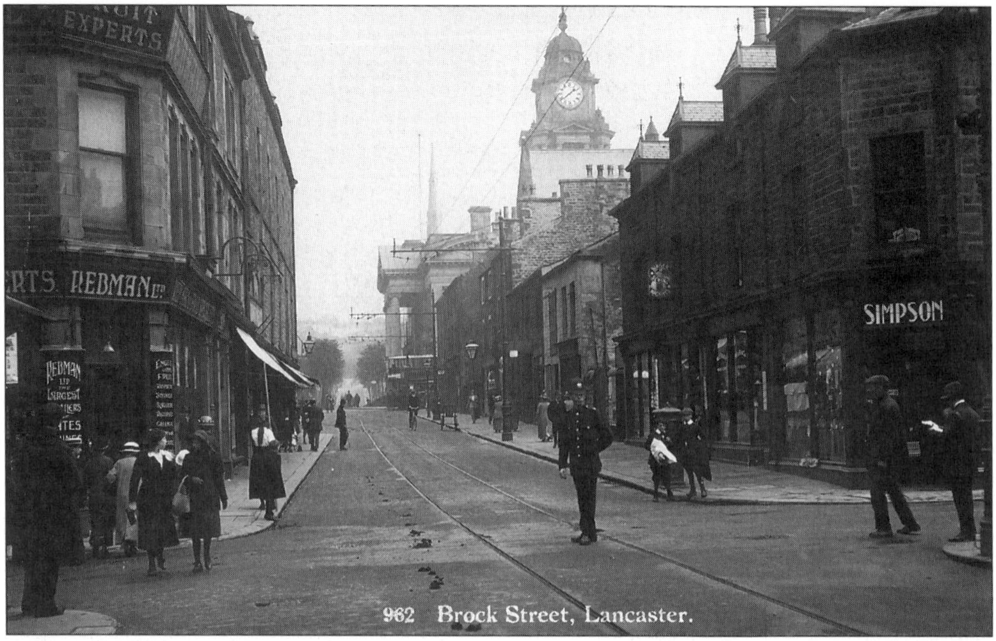

BROCK STREET, LANCASTER, looking in the direction of Dalton Square and the new Town Hall, on a postcard with the postmark 1917. Redmans are the occupants of the premises which formerly housed Boots the Chemist's (see page 102). Redmans were noted as a high quality fruit store, with a particularly fine selection of soft fruit.

BROCK STREET, LANCASTER, viewed from Dalton Square, with Lancaster Corporation Tramways' open top car No. 12, en route to Castle Station, at centre stage. The hoardings on the right hand side include one advertising the Alexandra Temperance Billiard Hall, which boasted twelve tables.

UNVEILING COVELLS CROSS, LANCASTER in 1902, showing, in the background, the Judges' Lodgings, once the home of Thomas Covell. Thomas Covell, who was six times Mayor of Lancaster, for 48 years Keeper of Lancaster Castle, and for 46 years one of the coroners of the county, died on 1 August 1639, and is buried at St Mary's, the Parish Church. The cross replaced an earlier cross, the remains of which stood on the same site.

A view of the JUDGES' LODGINGS, Lancaster, postmarked 1921 and published by T. Turner of Skipton. Once the house of Thomas Covell, it later became the home of the Coles of Beaumont Cote, who were responsible for substantial rebuilding and for extending the house. In 1825 it was purchased by Lancaster Corporation to provide lodgings for Judges attending quarterly assizes. The Judges' Lodgings were previously in Stonewell.

FRIEND'S MEETING HOUSE, LANCASTER, built in 1677 as a place of worship by the Society of Friends (Quakers). The registration of Quaker meeting places was illegal until the Act of Toleration towards nonconformists in 1689; prior to this date Quakers suffered much persecution. The doors to the Meeting House were at times locked, on the orders of the Mayor. At such times Friends would either meet in the lane outside the Meeting House or in members' homes.

A postcard of DALTON SQUARE, LANCASTER, posted in 1905. The memorial lamp, in the memory of Thomas Johnson, was later removed and erected in Stonewell, where it can still be seen. The photograph pre-dates the building of the new Town Hall. On this site stood Nazareth House, donated by Miss Coulston to the Sisters-of-Nazareth, an order of nuns. The corner of Nazareth House can be seen on the right hand side of the photograph.

CABLE STREET, looking west, with splendid views of both the Parish Church and Castle. Housing on the left hand side of Cable Street was demolished prior to the building of the bus station.

ST NICHOLAS STREET, LANCASTER, c. 1903, demolished during the 1960s to make way for a new shopping arcade. The shop on the right hand side of the photograph is that of F.H. Hewertson, jeweller. The shop also sold spectacles and eye glasses. Further down the road, at No. 29 St Nicholas' Street, was Fleming's, selling daily and evening newspapers. Next door to Flemings was the shop of C. Whiteside, the hairdresser.

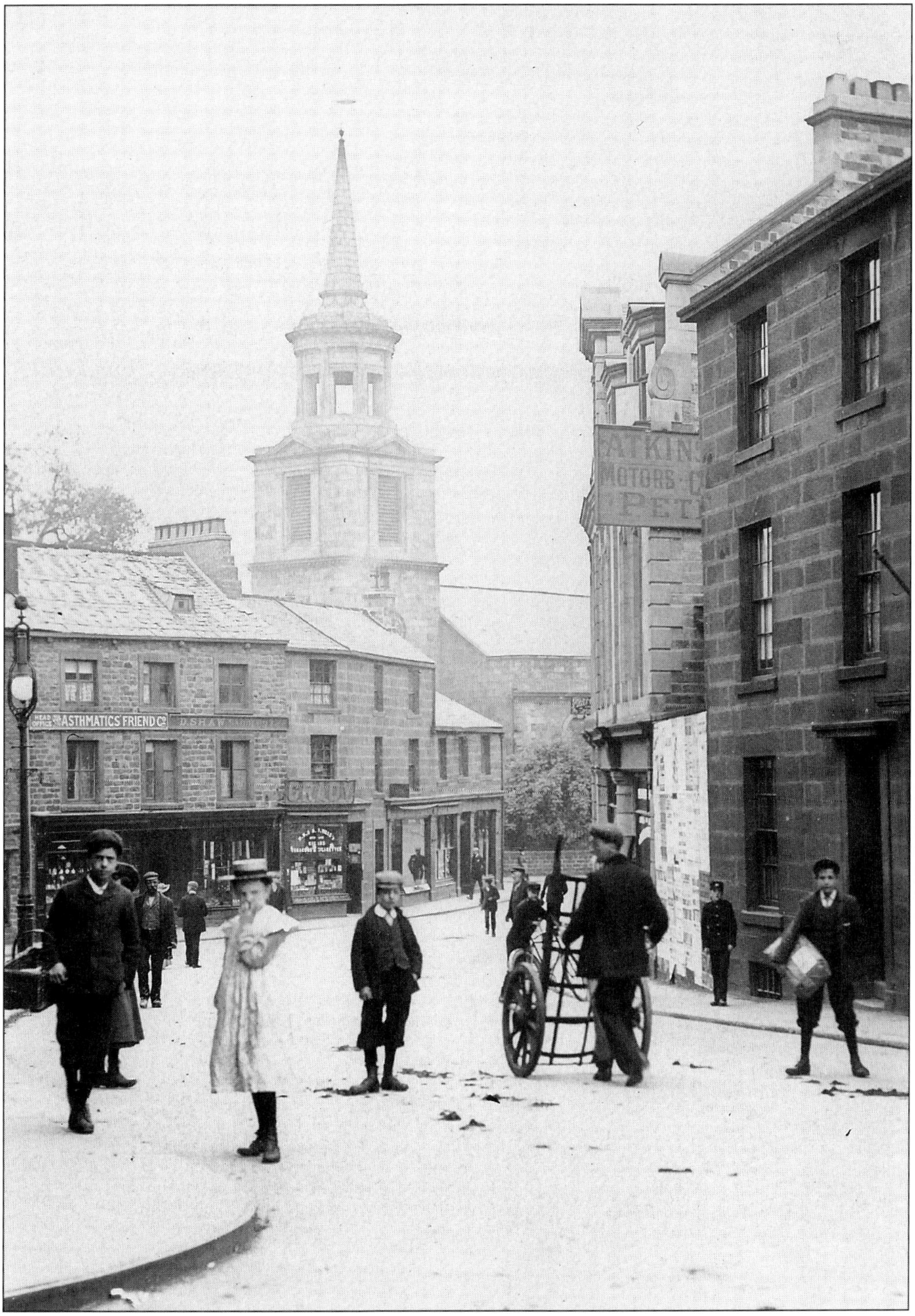

NORTH ROAD, LANCASTER. The name given to the street, which had just been made, was decided at a meeting of the Police Commissioners in 1843. Suggestions had included "New Street", "North Road" and "Police Folly". Another proposal was that it be called "Lower Cheapside", but it was finally decided that it should be called North Road.

STONEWELL, LANCASTER, with Singleton's Supply Stores on the left of the photograph, and the horse drawn tram arriving at the terminus in Stonewell. The tram service run by the Lancaster and District Tramways Company covered the route from Stonewell through Torrisholme to Morecambe. It is said that at times the pace was so leisurely that boys would alight and run alongside in order to relieve the boredom.

STONEWELL, LANCASTER and St Nicholas Street, demolished and now a shopping centre. In the centre of the photograph, the premises of Singleton's Supply Stores, shown on the previous page, have become Barrow, the boot manufacturer. The trams were originally double-deck, but some of them were altered to single-deck open cars, as shown above.

A view of HUBERT TERRACE, LANCASTER, on a postcard posted in 1907, representing the optimistic photographer who hoped to sell postcards to the residents. Evelyn manages not only to appear centre stage, but succeeds in persuading her parents to purchase the card. To avoid any doubt, she identifies her address at No. 15 and herself – as "me".

BLADES STREET, LANCASTER, photographed in 1905 – a scene never to be witnessed again, for although car parking is restricted to residents, the street today is jammed with vehicles. The two trees shown on the photograph have been felled, and a children's playground is located on the site.

THE SKERTON HOTEL. The hotel was one of many beer houses in Lancaster in the nineteenth century, each brewing their own ale. During the 1950s substantial interior alterations to the hotel were undertaken. The eighteenth-century doorway was transferred to a new position, and the door on the right removed and replaced by a window.

Three

Lancaster People and Places

TOWN HALL SQUARE, HIGH SHERIFF'S DAY, 6 JULY 1904.

ENTRY OF THE HIGH SHERIFF, 6 July 1904. The state entry of Mr Herbert Storey as the High Sheriff of Lancashire created more than the usual amount of interest, as he was only the second Lancaster-born man to have held the office in 100 years, the previous High Sheriff having been Lord Ashton, appointed in 1885. The High Sheriff and Mrs Storey received guests on the day at their home at Bailrigg prior to the ceremonial procession, the route of which was crowded with people. Numerous triumphal arches were erected, and the arches at Scotforth (right) and Penny Street (below) indicate the interest shown on the day.

Opposite: GEORGE WHITEHEAD, WHOLESALE AND RETAIL TOBACCONIST. Few shops in Lancaster show less change than George Whitehead's tobacconist's shop, at 139 St Leonardgate. Photographed in 1905, the shop window advertises F. and J. Smith's Gold Medal Glasgow Mixture and Wild Geranium Cigarettes.

ENTRY OF THE HIGH SHERIFF, 6 July 1904. The archway shown above is in Market Street, alongside the old Town Hall. The High Sheriff was escorted from his residence at Bailrigg, to take up his first duty at Lancaster Assizes. A body of javelin men were in attendance, a reminder of the times when the High Sheriff was personally responsible for the safety of judges for the time they were within his boundary.

LORD ROBERTS' ARRIVAL AT THE TOWN HALL, LANCASTER. Field Marshal Earl Roberts V.C. visited Lancaster on Thursday 29 July 1904 to dedicate the King's Own Royal Lancaster Regiment (popularly known as "the Fourth") Memorial Chapel which had been added to the Lancaster Parish Church. The Chapel was built in memory of the officers and men who died in the South African War. He unveiled a bronze tablet recording the names of the 282 who fell in battle. Lord Roberts arrived from Durham at Castle Station the previous evening, and was presented with the freedom of the city.

LORD ROBERTS INSPECTS THE GUARD OF HONOUR. The assembled guard of honour was inspected by Lord Roberts on his arrival at the Town Hall. Lord Roberts and General Cameron can be seen on the left in the foreground. Immediately behind them are Colonel Fitzherbert and General Borrett. Colonel Murray and Captain Parker are in the background.

LORD ROBERTS ENTERS THE TOWN HALL after inspecting the guard of honour.

THE MAYOR AND CORPORATION LEAVE THE TOWN HALL. Following the inspection of the guard of honour by Lord Roberts, the Mayor and Corporation left the Town Hall for the service at the Parish Church. Holy Communion had been celebrated at 8.00am and the dedication service, which was held at 11.30am, was conducted by the Lord Bishop of Manchester, Dr Knox.

LORD ROBERTS LEAVING THE TOWN HALL for the dedication service at the Parish Church. Following the service, Lord Roberts proceeded to Bowerham Barracks, where the officers entertained him to lunch.

MARKET HALL, LANCASTER. The completion of the covered market in 1846 was celebrated by a dinner at the Town Hall. The cost of the market hall was around £1,600 against an original estimate of between £800 and £900. The opening, which had been long awaited, was heralded as a most successful venture by the Corporation. As early as 1822, proposals to move the fish market from Market Street to a site between Anchor Lane and Chancery Lane, were under consideration. The Town Council also approved, early in 1845, the removal of the butter market from under the Town Hall to some vacant shops in the Shambles, in order to provide more accommodation for the grain market.

LANCASTER REGATTA, 1904. The first Lancaster Regatta took place on the River Lune in 1842. There were sailing, rowing and sculling matches. The Regatta which took place on 1 August 1904 was held on Halton Water, and the large number of spectators were entertained by the Yeomanry Band. Mr H. Simpson acted as judge and umpire and Mr W. Hoyle officiated as starter. The trial stakes for youths under 19 years of age attracted four entries, and the winner was W. Brockbank of Red Rose. Three boats entered the Borough Cup, for which the first prize was £10 with silver medals, the winners to give £2 to the second boat. The *Duchess* crew, winners by 7 to 8 lengths, were W.H. Winder, John Cutts, J. Suart, T.T. Hoggarth and E. Cutts (cox). Red Rose were also successful in the Lancaster Witch Stakes and the two oared race, in which they were represented by Jas. Cutts and S. Gunson. After the event, a dinner was held in the evening, at the Sun Inn.

LANCASTER FIRE BRIGADE, photographed by Robert Davis of 45 Coulston Road, Lancaster. The date of the photograph is not known, but it is not improbable that it was taken in 1906 when firemen representing 138 fire brigades were in Lancaster for the 31st annual meeting of the Fire Brigades' Friendly Society. This was their second visit to Lancaster, a previous annual meeting having been held there in 1894. There were almost 1,000 firemen present and, following a luncheon given for the officers by the Mayor, they marched from Dalton Square, along Thurnham Street, Penny Street, Market Street, Meeting House Lane, Station Road and West Road to the Giant Axe Field, where the afternoon was spent in various competitions.

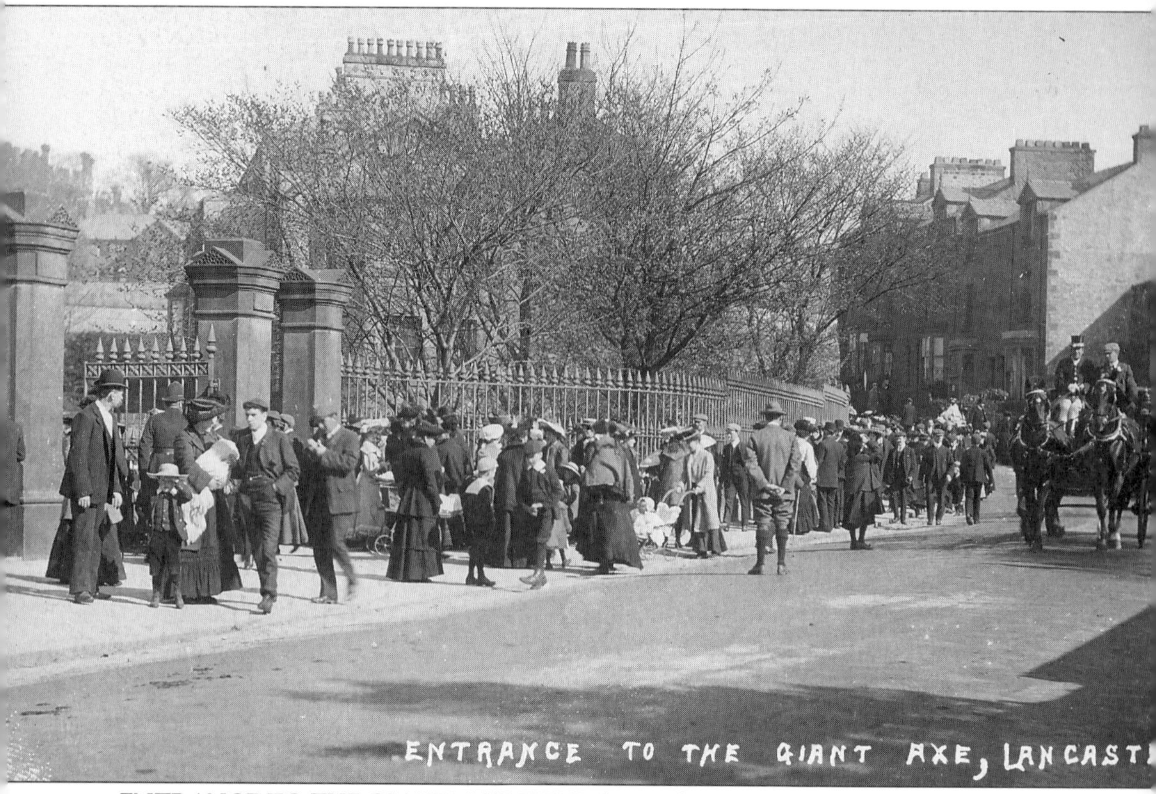

ENTRANCE TO THE GIANT AXE FIELD, 1906. The Lancaster Sports, traditionally held at Whitsuntide, had been run for twenty years by the Lancaster Amateur Athletic Association. In 1906, however, they reverted to a series of professional events, of which wrestling was a major attraction. Promoted by Mr G. Loxam, and in spite of good weather, it was soon apparent that the support was substantially less than in previous years. On Whit Monday the attendance was estimated at 3,000, barely half the normal attendance. The organisation was soon found to be lacking, as many of the entrants did not participate. Only 9 starters out of 31 entries for the half mile handicap flat race went to the starting line. The spectators were well satisfied with this event. G.B. Tincler of America, running from scratch, won a most thrilling race.

Opposite: LANCASTER HARRIERS VS SUTTON HARRIERS. On 9 January 1909 a combined team of Lancaster Primrose, Friends, and Skerton Harriers met Sutton Harriers and Athletic Club over an 8½ mile course through Scotforth to Thurnham, returning along Cockerham Road to the Royal Infirmary. Sutton, ex-national champions, were to prove too strong on the day, in what was a close finish. The first five to complete the course for Lancaster were J.R. Hall (Primrose), 53 minutes, 58 seconds (6th), A. Gardner (Friends) (7th), J. Ellwood (8th), J.E. Towers (9th), J. Robinson (11th), T. Parkinson (12th).

BOUNDARY RIDERS, LANCASTER, 1907. The riding of the boundary, an event taking place every seven years, was in 1907 supported by fewer members of the public than in earlier times. Landowners over whose land the 14½ mile route passed had requested that only the flagman and two assistants cover the entire boundary. The general public kept to the roads and gathered first at Beaumont Bridge to hear the proclamation, "Oyez, Oyez, Oyez. This is the boundary mark of the Borough of Lancaster, known by the name of Beaumont Bridge. God save the King."

FLOODS AT LANCASTER, 17 MARCH 1907. The floods which occurred in March 1907 were probably the most destructive ever witnessed in Lancaster and district. The combination of continuous rain during Saturday and gales that night and in the early hours of Sunday produced a tide estimated at 29 feet and caused water to overflow the Quay alongside Damside Street, as far as Stonewell. There was great concern for the safety of the inmates of the Sanatorium, which could be seen to be surrounded by water. Dr Parker, the Medical Officer of Health, was roused, and after discussion with Chief Constable Harriss, drew up plans to evacuate the inmates by boat. Around 4.30am the water started to subside, and an omnibus and two horses were chartered from the County Hotel. Dr Parker and the Chief Constable approached within hailing distance and to their relief were assured by the Matron that the inmates had been evacuated to an upper storey, and were in no immediate danger.The water level had dropped by midday, Sunday, and the patients were rescued. The entire building had been surrounded by water to a depth of not less than seven feet. Water had penetrated the building to a depth of three feet, and the force of it had lifted the floor of the scarlatina ward twelve inches in two places.

FLOODS, SANATORIUM, LANCASTER.

FLOODS, MARSH, LANCASTER, 1907. The continuous rain had swollen the rivers to such a level that, when met by the spring tide, the River Lune, already bank high, burst its banks in several places. All the land on the marshes between Lancaster and Morecambe was flooded to a depth of several feet. Almost three quarters of a mile of post and rail fencing along the Glasson railway was washed down. The railway line was flooded, and twelve or more inches of ballast from under the rails was washed away. A temporary bus service ran between Lancaster and Glasson, and 150 men employed to make good the damage to the permanent way worked to such effect that the line was re-opened on Tuesday.

THE ATHENAEUM THEATRE DESTROYED, FEBRUARY 1908. The theatre, built in 1781 by Austin and Whitlock, was financed partly by subscriptions of eight shares of £50 each. Interest of 5 per cent was paid to the subscribers, who were also given a free ticket of admission for the season. The fire, which took place on Saturday evening, almost completely destroyed the Athenaeum Theatre. An audience of schoolchildren had attended a matinée performance of Mr Peter Thompson's *Babes in the Wood* pantomime, and had fortunately left the theatre before the fire broke out. The damage to the theatre was estimated at about £4,000 and, regrettably, the insurance cover at the time was for only about half that amount. The rebuilding of the theatre commenced almost immediately, and it re-opened in September 1908, under its new name, The Grand Theatre. The group of actors shown below are photographed outside the Grand Theatre, alongside a placard announcing "The enormous success of Stock Coy".

LABOUR DEMONSTRATION, LANCASTER, 30 JUNE 1906. The demonstration, organised by the Lancaster Trades and Labour Council and the Lancaster Branch of the Independent Labour Party, was billed as in recognition of "Labour Day". On the Friday evening prior to the demonstration a mass meeting was held at the Co-operative Hall. Speakers at the meeting included Mr George N. Barnes, M.P. and General Secretary of the Amalgamated Society of Engineers, and Mr J.R. Clynes M.P. George Barnes had defeated Mr Bonar Law in a three cornered contest in the parliamentary election for the Blackfriars Division of Glasgow. The meeting was attended by a large and enthusiastic audience.

WILLIAM SMITH FESTIVAL, LANCASTER, MARCH 1910. William Smith (1849-1913) was the Liberal M.P. for North Lonsdale Division from 1892 to the dissolution of Parliament in 1895. He generously made provision for a gala for the children, to be held at Easter time. Toys were distributed to all children under seven years of age, either at school or in the market, and in 1910 about 7,000 toys were provided as souvenirs of the festival. A football competition, held in the morning for the elementary schools, was won by St Thomas's, who defeated St Mary's in the final. The attendance was estimated at between 15,000 and 20,000, and the event was blessed with brilliant weather. The maypole dance shown above was by the children of Halton School, trained by Miss Bateman, and by the children of Caton School, under the direction of Miss Child. Sports were organised for boys and girls, and the boys of Bowerham School were the winners of a tug-of-war competition for boys representing elementary schools. The festival concluded with a display of Japanese daylight fireworks given by Messrs Pain and Sons of London, and with dancing to the music of the Lancaster Borough Band.

MORRIS DANCERS, WILLIAM SMITH FESTIVAL, LANCASTER, MARCH 1910.

RIGIIT HONOURABLE SIR HENRY BANNERMAN M.P., N.W. HELME ESQ., M.P., AND WHITLEY THOMPSON ESQ. on the occasion of the visit of the leader of the Liberal Party to Lancaster. Norval W. Helme, Chairman of the Lancaster Liberal Association and a staunch supporter of the Wesleyan Methodist Church, was elected M.P. for Lancaster in 1900, defeating Colonel William Henry Foster of Hornby Castle, the sitting M.P., by 44 votes. He was knighted in the Birthday Honours list of 1912 and served as M.P. until 1918, when he lost his seat to General A. Hunter.

SKERTON WESLEY BROTHERHOOD CHOIR, photographed in 1908 when competition between choirs was extremely keen. Featured in the photograph are John Thomas Stilling (back row, far right) and his brother Edward Stilling (third row, far right), the latter a stonemason by trade who resided on Lune Street, Skerton.

LANCASTER MOOR HOSPITAL ORCHESTRA, photographed c. 1912. The violinist seated front row, third from the right, is Ernest Vernon, a male attendant at Lancaster Asylum. He was the first registered psychiatric nurse to be enrolled at Lancaster.

LANCASTER SWIMMING CLUB, 1912 and 1918. In 1912 membership of the Lancaster Swimming Club was 130 (53 ladies, 77 gentlemen), a decrease of 68 against the previous year. The schools squadron competition was won by the Boys' National School, the junior championship by A. Gerrard, the ladies' championship by Miss N. Kittson, the ten lengths championship of Lancaster by R.H. Wilcock, and the championship of the Lune by G. Fox. The polo team, under the captaincy of J. Eaglesfield, won five matches and lost five in the Northern Water Polo League, scoring 30 goals against 24. They reached the final in the County Competition, losing to Wigan. A club photograph, taken in 1918, is shown below.

LANCASTER SALVATION ARMY BAND, 1912. Drawn from all sections of the community, the Salvation Army is known for its sterling work for the underprivileged. Featured in the above are: standing third from the right, Mr Willcocks; fourth from the right, Mr A.J. Holmes (with cornet), a well-known painter and decorator from Vincent Street; seated second from the right, Mr Cragg (bass). The bandmaster seated in the centre is Mr Bateman, whose shoe repair shop was on Aberdeen Road.

LANCASTER SALVATION ARMY BAND, 1935. Photographed in Dalton Square, in front of the Victoria Memorial, the band members are as follows, seated from the left: Mr Edward Holmes, Mr G. Allen, Mr Herbert Moorhouse, Major Walker, Adjutant Ogle, Mr Bram Taylor, Mr W. Cragg, Mr A. Reginald Holmes, son of Mr A.J. Holmes, who is in the 1912 photograph above. Standing from the left: Mr Arnold Cragg, Mr Tom Bradley, Mr Ronnie Allen, Mr G. Allen, Mr W. Searle, Mr Cyril France, bandmaster, Mr Walter Taylor, Mr A. Butler, Mr Wealden, Mr Moorhouse, Mr Arnold France, Mr William Raine and Mr Denis Raine. Older Lancastrians will recall the hut next to the Picturedrome Cinema in Lower Church Street which the band used for rehearsing.

HIS MAJESTY THE KING VISITS LANCASTER, 24 AUGUST 1912. King George V arrived at Lancaster on Monday 19 August 1912 to stay at Abbeystead House, the guest of the Earl of Sefton. On Saturday his coach proceeded at a slow pace along Greaves Road, South Road, and Thurnham Street, to the main entrance of the Town Hall in Dalton Square. Members of the Corporation of Lancaster and Morecambe, County and Borough Magistrates, and members of public bodies were on the platform to greet his arrival. The 5th Battalion of the King's Own Regiment formed the guard of honour in Dalton Square, shown in the postcard below.

KING GEORGE V'S VISIT TO LANCASTER, 24 AUGUST 1912. After the presentation, the King's carriage proceeded along Brock Street, Penny Street and Market Street. The carriage stopped in Market Square, where 4,000 schoolchildren sang two verses of the national anthem. The streets along which the royal cortège passed were lined by representatives of all the Battalions of the King's Own Regiment, Boy Scouts, and the National Reserve. The King is seen acknowledging the traditional salute given by the Boy Scouts.

JOHN CORKILL AND SONS, BAKERS AND CONFECTIONERS, LANCASTER. The surname Corkill and its association with baking and confectionery in Lancaster goes back as far as 1881, when Edward Corkill of Quine and Corkill had a shop at 97 Penny Street. Thomas Edward Corkill, a baker, had a shop at 58 Penny Street between 1885 and 1890, and Thomas Edward Corkill junior a shop at 40 Coulston Road. John Corkill's premises in 1901 were at 24 Prospect Street and, by 1934, at Brook Street.

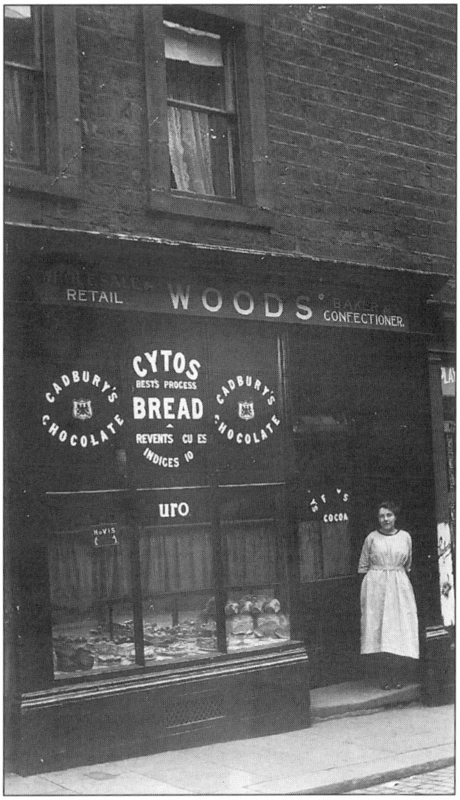

JAMES A. WOODS, HIGH CLASS BAKER AND CONFECTIONER, 119 ST LEONARD GATE. The baker's shop, demolished in the 1950s, was formerly occupied at the turn of the century by Mr W.H. Corlett. Thomas Woods, wholesale and retail baker and confectioner, was established at the premises no later than 1912. The delivery vehicle shown below, photographed standing in Ellithorn's Yard alongside the shop, was in all probability the first in service bearing the name of James Woods. The plans for redevelopment of the site have not come to fruition and the area now serves as a car park.

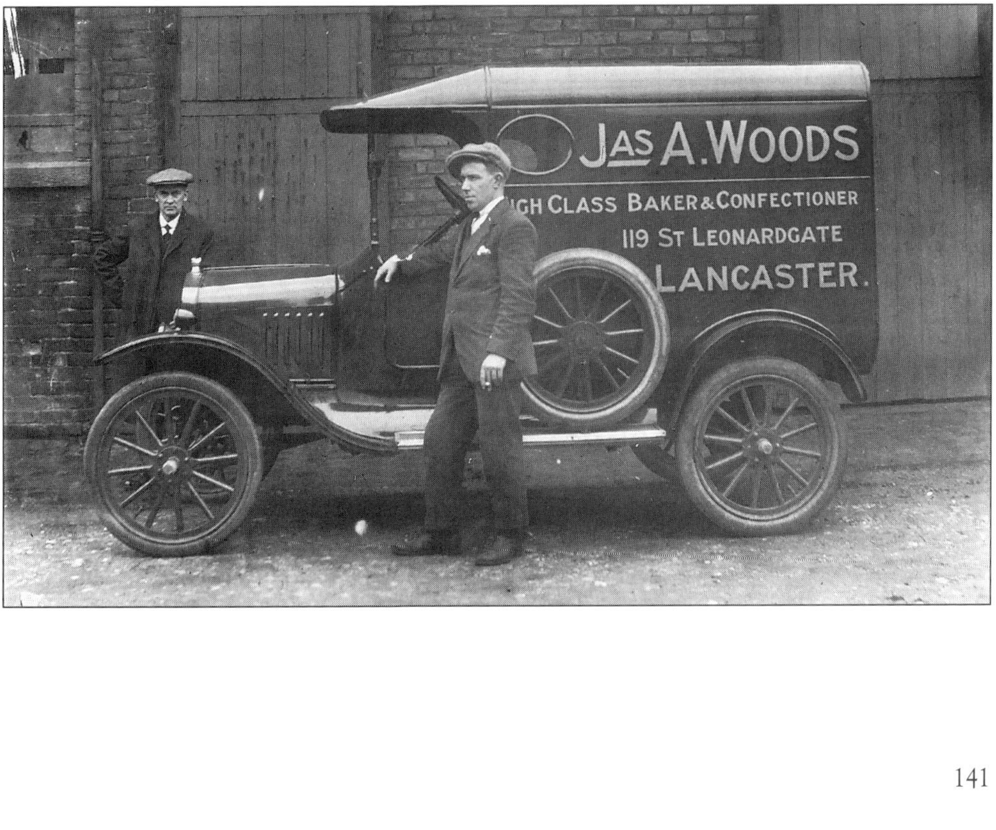

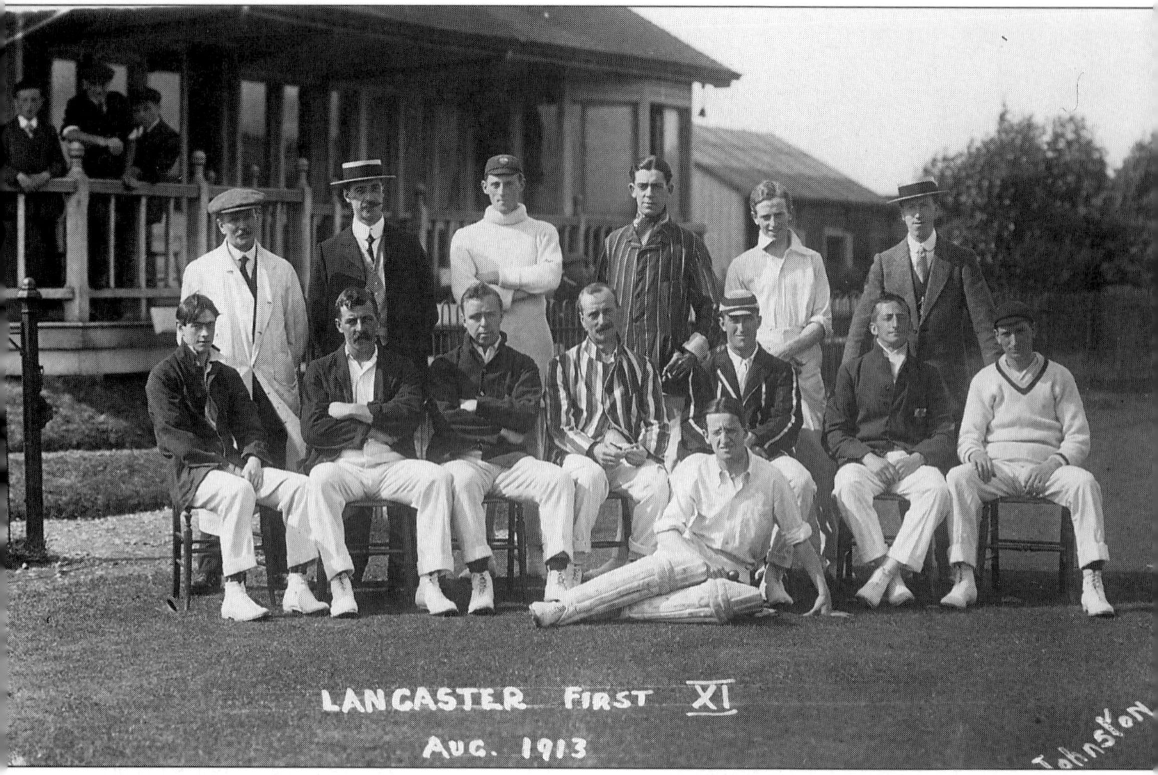

LANCASTER CRICKET CLUB FIRST ELEVEN, AUGUST 1913. August 1913 was the month selected for Tom Iddon's benefit. Iddon had been the club professional since 1900, and during that period Lancaster were champions of the North Lancashire League in 1900, 1901, 1903, 1906 and 1907. His finest performance was in 1907 against Millom, when he took all ten wickets, conceding only twenty one runs. His benefit match was against Bolton and, due to the late arrival of their train, the start was delayed until 3.20pm. Lancaster won the toss and elected to bat. They declared with the score at 162 runs for 8 wickets, thanks mainly to J.S. Punchard, who scored 61 not out. Bolton were reeling and facing defeat but, with their score at 86 runs for 6 wickets, bad light followed by heavy rain caused the match to be abandoned.

REV. HAROLD HASTINGS M.A., MASTER OF LANCASTER PAGEANT, AUGUST 1913. The Lancaster Pageant, held in August 1913, consisted of ten episodes selected to represent important historical events. They included the visits of King John and John of Gaunt, the founding of the Grammar School, the wars with the Scots, the trial of the Lancashire witches and the Jacobite rebellions, all of significance in the history of the town. A cast of two thousand, drawn from all walks of life, were involved, and large audiences, paying from one shilling for a standing position to twenty one shillings for a reserved and covered seat, watched the performances.

MRS TOWNHOPE, LANCASTER PAGEANT. Mrs Townhope, the wife of Colonel Townhope, played by Mrs A.N. Benson and handsomely dressed in green and gold brocade, prepares to enter her coach. She travels to greet Bonnie Prince Charlie on his arrival at the Market Place, Lancaster in 1745. Her husband, one of the first Englishmen to support the Scots, has joined the Prince on the road between Shap and Kendal. Mrs Benson, the wife of Dr Benson of Meadowside, was trained at the Guildhall College of Music and sang professionally with the D'Oyly Carte Opera Company.

BONNIE PRINCE CHARLIE, LANCASTER PAGEANT. The scene depicted is the second Jacobite rising in 1745, and the entry of Prince Charles Edward, played by Rev. Harold Hastings, into Lancaster at the head of his Highland troops.

LANCASTER PAGEANT, 1745. The Trustees of Ripley Hospital kindly agreed to the use of Springfield Park as the setting for the Pageant. The final episode, which commences with the entry into Lancaster by Prince Charles Edward and the proclamation at the Market Cross of his father James as king, concludes with the retreat of the Prince from Derby, through Lancaster, pursued by the Hanoverian troops led by the Duke of Cumberland and General Oglethorpe. The crowd dispersed slowly after this final episode, which is followed by a grand finale and march past of all performers.

LANCASTER PAGEANT – KING CHARLES II. Episode Eight of the Pageant shows Charles, King of the Scots, passing through Lancaster on 11 August 1651. On his journey south, Charles, here played by Mr A. Edwards, stayed the night at Ashton Hall. He was to be defeated at Worcester on 3 September 1651.

THE PAGEANT BAND. The music for the Pageant was arranged by a committee under the chairmanship of Mr J.W. Aldous, M.A., with Mr C.H. Hamer of 56A Regent Street the Honorary Secretary. The music for the Song of Lancaster, *The Pageant Passes*, was written by Mr Aldous, and the words by Mr G.A. Stocks, M.A.

THE PALS COMPANY CHURCH PARADE, LANCASTER, 6 SEPTEMBER 1914. The commencement of the First World War in 1914 saw the formation of "Pals Companies", with men enlisting in the armed forces in the hope of an early cessation of hostilities. The photograph shows the "Pals" leaving the Parish Church after the morning service. The vicar, the Reverend J.U.N. Bardsley, marched with the men back to the Drill Hall in Phoenix Street. They reassembled at the Drill Hall at 6.30pm and, led by Major Bates and Captain Seward, marched through crowded streets to Castle Station. The men were in cheerful spirits as they said their "goodbyes" to relatives at the station. The Mayor and Mayoress were present to bid the men God speed.

PLEA FOR CONTRIBUTIONS TO ASSIST PRISONERS OF WAR. The hopes for an early end to the war were not to be realised. Reports of men either killed or missing appeared weekly in the *Lancaster Guardian*. A thought for those reported as prisoners of war is conveyed by the sign on the donkey cart, asking passers by to spare a penny for comforts for the prisoners of war of the Loyal North Lancashire Regiment.

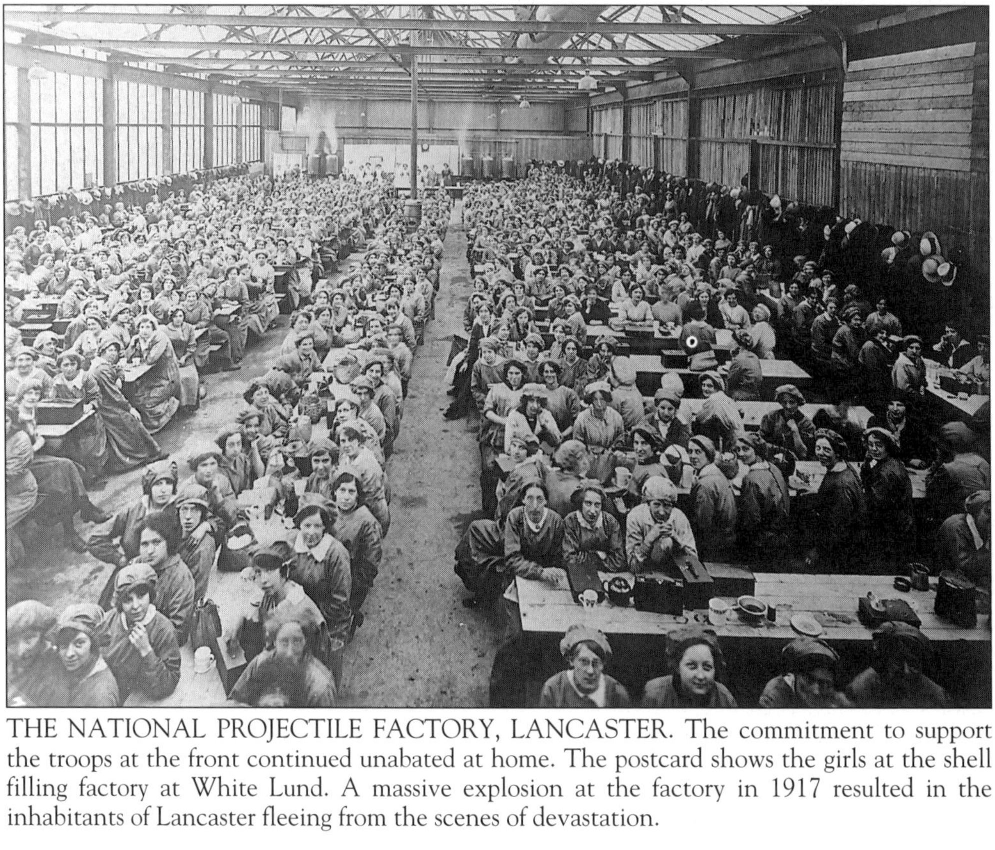

THE NATIONAL PROJECTILE FACTORY, LANCASTER. The commitment to support the troops at the front continued unabated at home. The postcard shows the girls at the shell filling factory at White Lund. A massive explosion at the factory in 1917 resulted in the inhabitants of Lancaster fleeing from the scenes of devastation.

LANCASTER DISCHARGED SOLDIERS MILITARY BAND, 9 JUNE 1919. The end of the war in 1918 saw the demobilisation of the forces and the return of men hoping to resume careers and enter employment. Many were to suffer unemployment in the depression following the war. The comradeship which had been formed during the war did not desert them in those difficult times.

DEEP CUTTING BRIDGE, LANCASTER. The bridge, which carries Ashton Road over the Lancaster Canal, illustrates the competence of the engineers responsible for its planning and construction. Approved by an Act of Parliament in 1792, its objective was for the carriage of limestone and slate from the north, and coal from the south. The route selected for the canal was nearly parallel with the turnpike road from Preston to Kendal.

PENNY'S HOSPITAL, KING STREET, LANCASTER. Founded in 1720, by the will of Alderman William Penny, the almshouses were built to provide accommodation for twelve poor men of Lancaster. The pump in the centre of the yard supplied water for the houses. The two houses nearest to King Street were demolished during road widening carried out in 1974. The remaining houses were at the same time modernised to provide more comfortable accommodation.

SKERTON ST LUKE'S CRICKET CLUB, 1924. Formed in 1924, St Luke's were commended at the end of the season for their undoubted enthusiasm. During the season they called on 22 players, of which 15 were to be utilised as bowlers. In their first match in Section C of the Lancaster and District Cricket League, they were dismissed by Warton for a total of five runs! Later in the season, T. Calkeld produced the impressive return of seven wickets for six runs in eight overs, against Halton Seconds. Halton were dismissed for 26 runs and St Luke's, in reply, fell just short of this total, scoring 23 runs.

THE ASYLUM, LANCASTER. The County Lunatic Asylum (Lancaster Moor Hospital) was opened 28 July 1816, following an Act of Parliament in 1807, "for the better care and maintenance of lunatics...". Enlarged several times, a large annexe was built on part of the old Lancaster Racecourse in 1882. The building in the background is the old Nursing Administration Block, which is currently not in use.

GALLERY 5A, COUNTY LUNATIC ASYLUM, LANCASTER. The above photograph was taken early this century, probably around 1907. Admissions had increased steadily since the opening in 1816, and first exceeded 1,000 in 1869. Devoted staff had none of today's methods of treatment available to them, and straight jackets and padded cells were often the order of the day. Developments in the use of drugs and electro-convulsive therapy treatment were to bring relief, and many patients were later to be seen walking about Lancaster.

WILLIAMSON PARK, LANCASTER, formerly the site of stone quarries on Lancaster Moor and covering an area of thirty eight acres. The first work on the park was carried out in the 1960s, when an unknown benefactor provided work for the unemployed in the construction of a drive and pathways. The development of the park, as it is today, was financed by Mr James Williamson (Snr), who employed Mr Maclean, a landscape architect from Castle Donnington, to design the layout of the park which included a waterfall and the lake shown above.

THE ENTRANCE GATES, WILLIAMSON PARK. The Park was to prove extremely popular with the local population. The electric tram service from Castle Station to Williamson Park, introduced in 1903, enabled people of all ages to enjoy the recreational facilities of the park.

THE OBSERVATORY, WILLIAMSON PARK, LANCASTER.

THE OBSERVATORY, WILLIAMSON PARK, LANCASTER. The observatory, now demolished, was built by the Corporation of Lancaster to house astronomical instruments presented by the mill owner Albert Greg Esq., J.P. of Escowbeck, Caton. It was opened by the Astronomer Royal of Scotland, Dr Copeland, on Friday 29 July 1892.

THE BAND PERFORMANCE, WILLIAMSON PARK. Band performances were a regular and popular feature in the park. The photograph was taken c. 1902, prior to the construction of the bandstand.

THE TEMPLE, WILLIAMSON PARK. The temple is an appropriate vantage point, and visitors are seen here being photographed when it was newly constructed. Now surrounded by shrubs and trees, it stands in a less frequented part of the park. Its commanding position provided extensive views of Lancaster, Morecambe Bay and the Lakeland mountains in the distance. The canopy has been demolished, leaving only the central column in situ.

THE PALM HOUSE, WILLIAMSON PARK. Although the park was handed over to the Corporation in 1881, development continued and the Palm House was one of a number of additions proposed in 1904. The dimensions of the Palm House are 72 feet long by 42 feet wide, and 44 feet high. It housed a collection of tropical flowering and foliage plants. The east wall, built in stone, was covered with tropical and sub-tropical climbing and flowering plants.

THE PALM HOUSE INTERIOR, WILLIAMSON PARK. All the plants in this photograph were destroyed by fire in 1949, and the building now houses a dazzling collection of butterflies.

THE ASHTON MEMORIAL, WILLIAMSON PARK, LANCASTER. Known locally as The Structure, and built 1907-1909, the memorial stands at the highest point of the park. Designed by John Belcher R.A., and costing £87,000, it is built in the neo-Classical style in Portland Stone, with the main staircase and balustrades in Cornish granite. Lancaster builders Waring and Gillow Ltd. were responsible for its construction; the author's great grandfather, John Edward Dowthwaite, was involved in the installation of the parquet floor.

NEW BRIDGE, WILLIAMSON PARK. A rustic style bridge was originally built over the lake. The stone bridge which took its place was one of the improvements initiated by Lord Ashton (James Williamson Jnr) in 1904.

LANCASTER CASTLE. Lancaster Castle is undoubtedly the attraction which draws many visitors to the city. Its commanding position, high above the River Lune, is an ideal vantage point for viewing the surrounding countryside. Although much of the castle is still in use as a prison, and access to that part is therefore denied to the public, there are plans for change which will at some future date permit it to be opened to the general public. In the meantime, the Shire Hall, built 1796-1798, is the major attraction. Hanging on the walls of the Hall are heraldic shields which include Coats of Arms of the High Sheriffs dating from 1129.

HANGING CORNER, LANCASTER CASTLE. Framed in the doorway of the pinioning room is the chair made in 1828 for Jane Scott. She was too weak to walk, and it was used to convey her to the public gallows which were erected facing the churchyard.

THE COURTYARD, LANCASTER CASTLE. The view no longer available to the general public is that of the inner courtyard, looking in the direction of the Gateway Tower. The Tower, strengthened c. 1400, was named after John O' Gaunt and a statue of him, carved by Claude Nimmo in the nineteenth century, was placed above the gateway entrance.

Acknowledgements

Recognition must first be accorded to late members of the Alston family who provided the initial stimulus by their reminiscences:

My great aunt Isabella (born 1880) for details of her childhood at Tarn Cottage, Bulk, and her schooldays at Halton,
My aunt Violet, for her schooldays at Hornby and adult life in Lancaster,
My father Robert, for his detailed descriptions of life in Lancaster at the beginning of this century, and also his recollections of Caton – the home of his maternal grandparents.

The friendliness of the inhabitants of the villages included in the book has been beyond expectation, and the contributions of the following have been of great assistance:

Stella Kenyon (Wray), David Hartnup (Wray), Clive Lamb (Hornby), Peter and Joyce Maudsley (Caton), George Gardner (Caton) and Bill Hosfield (Halton).

The readers of my weekly column in the *Lancaster Guardian* have at times provided unexpected information, and to them I must place on record my appreciation.

I would also like to thank:

The staff of Lancaster Reference Library, particularly Susan Wilson and Alan Duckworth (much of the material relating to Lancaster has been obtained from the library's records),
Frank Alston, for identification of my distant cousins on a mystery photograph (page 6) which has been in my possession some thirty years.
My friend Ernst Sussman for the photographs of the British Rail list of Tolls (page 74) and of the Toll Bar (page 75),
My wife, Dr Jean Alston, for support and assistance with the fieldwork.